Kaleidoscope

Level B

Columbus, Ohio

The McGraw-Hill Companies

Unit Themes

UNIT **1** **Friendship**

UNIT **2** **City Wildlife**

UNIT **3** **Imagination**

UNIT **4** **Storytelling**

UNIT **5** **Money**

UNIT **6** **Country Life**

UNIT **2** City Wildlife

Table of Contents

Table of Contents

Table of Contents

Table of Contents

Home before Dark

by Rosalie Koskimaki
illustrated by Sally Schaedler

Every day after school they played baseball.
They played until it began to get dark. Then it
was dinnertime and time to go home.

One day the baseball rolled away. "I've lost
my new ball," Peter said.

"I'm sorry," said Robert. "I have to go home."
"I'll be late," Elizabeth said.

Kate thought to herself: *Mother and Dad said to be home before dinnertime. But Peter looks sad.*

"I'll help you!" Kate said.

They looked and looked. At last they found the ball.

Kate ran home. Her father and mother were waiting outside. "You're late," they said. "Are you all right?"

Kate told them about the baseball. And they were not angry!

Kate had helped Peter.

Shadow Friends

by Carolyn Gloeckner
illustrated by Len Epstein

The sun was like fire over the desert. No breeze blew. The cool mountains were far away. The ant needed shade.

It met a toad. "Come into my shadow," said the toad. "You will be cooler."

The ant did so. The toad hopped off across the sand. The ant followed in the toad's shadow. They headed for the mountains.

They met a fox. "Come, toad! Cool off in my shadow," said the fox.

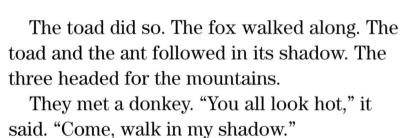

The toad did so. The fox walked along. The toad and the ant followed in its shadow. The three headed for the mountains.

They met a donkey. "You all look hot," it said. "Come, walk in my shadow."

The fox did so. All four went toward the mountains.

It grew hotter. "I can go no farther," said the donkey. Just then a shadow fell over them— the mountain's shadow.

They soon found water. They drank and rested. And ever since, they have been the best of friends.

The Friendship Box

by Marsha Moss

illustrated by Lane Gregory

Kim's mom brought in the mail. She found something for Kim.

"Look, Kim," she said. "You got a card."

Kim opened it and read it.

"Who is it from?" Mom asked.

"It's from Ron," Kim said. "He invited me to his birthday party."

"That will be fun," Mom said. "After all, Ron is your best friend."

Kim didn't look very happy.

"Why are you sad?" Mom asked.

"I don't know what to give him," Kim said. "Don is getting him fish. Tom will get him a game. Those are good gifts. But I want to get him a really good present. After all, I'm his best friend."

"I know what you can do," Mom said.

"What's that?" Kim asked.

"Make a friendship box," Mom said.

"A friendship box? What's that?" Kim asked.

"Take an empty box," Mom explained. "Fill it with things you make on your own."

Kim liked the idea. She got started right away. Kim knew how to knit. So she decided to knit Ron a hat. Kim also knew how to paint with wax. So Kim made a picture of Ron and herself.

Soon Kim was done with the picture. She let the wet wax dry. Then she put the picture inside the box. Next she put in the hat. The gifts fit well. Last she added yellow paper outside the box.

Kim took the friendship box to the party. Ron opened each gift. Everyone clapped when Ron opened the friendship box.

"Thanks, Kim," Ron said later. "I liked all my gifts. But your gifts were the best. I'm glad we're best friends!"

Sam and Mr. Stone

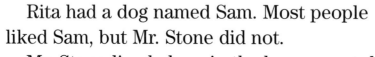

by Abby Northanger
illustrated by Brock Nicol

Rita had a dog named Sam. Most people liked Sam, but Mr. Stone did not.

Mr. Stone lived alone in the house next door to Rita. His nephew came once in a while. Most of the time, though, Mr. Stone was by himself. Rita never saw him smile. Mr. Stone was always grumbling and complaining. He said Sam made too much noise.

Every morning Rita went to school. Sam stayed home alone. One afternoon Rita came home. Sam was standing outside. The flowers by the window were wrecked. They were broken and scattered all over.

"Bad dog!" Rita shouted. "You should be inside the house. How did you get out?" She wrapped her arms around Sam.

Mr. Stone was watching Rita and Sam. "The dog saw a gopher and jumped out of the open window," Mr. Stone said. "He's not bad. He's just lonely."

Rita looked at Mr. Stone. She had an idea. "Could you keep Sam with you?" she asked. "Just when I'm at school?"

Mr. Stone looked surprised. "I guess I wouldn't mind," he said. Then he smiled.

Friends Forever

by Sally George
illustrated by Deborah White

Judy and Maria were friends. One day, Maria got mad at Judy for tearing a page in Maria's book. They yelled at each other. Judy was sad and trudged home. It wasn't far. Judy's eyes were blurry with tears as she walked.

Judy's father saw her crying. "What happened?" he asked.

Judy sobbed, "Maria yelled at me. We had a huge fight. Now we won't be friends."

"Why do you say that?" her father asked.

"It was a huge, giant fight. It made my stomach churn. We're both mad," Judy said.

"And now you're both sad," he said. He wiped the tears and smudges off her face.

"Do you think Maria is sad, too?" Judy asked. "Then I'll try to be her friend again."

"That's a good idea," her father said. "Maybe she will try, too."

Judy wanted to do something nice for Maria. She decided to make fudge. She was excited as she stirred the batter.

The next day Judy met Maria. "I was sad after we yelled at each other," Judy said.

"I was, too," Maria said.

"Let's be friends again," Judy said. Judy gave Maria the fudge, and they each had a piece. It worked like magic.

Maria smiled and said, "We'll always be friends. Friends can get mad, too."

"Just as long as they make up," Judy said. "Being mad isn't fun."

Good Friends

by James A. Schulz
illustrated by John Kanzler

Turtle and Elephant were good friends. It wasn't easy, but they kept trying.

One day, Elephant said, "Let's go for a walk."

Turtle said, "I can't keep up with you, and you'll probably step on my head."

"Don't worry!" said Elephant. "I'll carry you with my trunk."

"Thank you for the favor. That would be quite nice," said Turtle.

So Elephant picked up Turtle and started off.

"Stop!" said Turtle.

"What's the matter?" said Elephant.

"I think we're lost," said Turtle.

"But I've only gone five steps," said Elephant.

"Well, I've never been this far before," said Turtle.

"Don't be such a coward," laughed Elephant.

Elephant started walking again. It was a beautiful day. The sky was the color of the blue, blue ocean.

"Stop!" cried Turtle.

"What now?" asked Elephant.

"I am quite out of breath and queasy from the speed," said Turtle.

"Just look straight ahead. I will try not to be so quick," said Elephant.

24

"I will look straight ahead," said Turtle quietly.

"Trust me," said Elephant. "I'll get you home safely. You're my friend."

"All right," said Turtle. "I will trust you. Let's go."

So they did go for a walk. They had a good time. Turtle and Elephant were good friends. It wasn't easy, but they kept trying.

Reading Reflections

These questions can help you think about the stories you have just read. After you write your responses, discuss them with a partner.

Focus on the Characters

- How are the title characters alike in "Sam and Mr. Stone"?
- In "Good Friends" why isn't it easy for Turtle and Elephant to be friends?
- Do you think Kate makes the right choice to help Peter in "Home before Dark"? Why or why not?

Focus on the Stories

- In "Home before Dark" Peter would have been unable to find his ball without the help of his friend Kate. Name another story in this unit in which friends help one another.
- The excitable dog Sam and the grumpy Mr. Stone seem like they would be an unlikely pair, but they become friends. Think of two other stories in this unit in which a surprise friendship develops.
- Which story in this unit is the best example of friendship? Explain your choice.

Focus on the Theme

- People show friendship in various ways. How do the characters in this unit demonstrate friendship?

- Friendship has its ups and downs. Turtle and Elephant in "Good Friends" realize they must keep trying in order to make their friendship work. Name a story in this unit in which characters overcome their differences so they can remain friends.

- In "The Friendship Box" Kim chooses gifts that she has made to put in the birthday box for her best friend, Ron. What would you put in a friendship box for your best friend? Explain your choices.

Good-bye, Baby Bird

by Colleen Darrow
illustrated by Meg Aubrey

Nora and Dad were at home. Suddenly, they saw something fall onto the balcony. It was small and dark.

"What was that?" Nora asked.

She ran to the balcony. Dad followed.

"Look, Dad!" Nora said. "It's a little bird!"

"It's just a baby," Dad said.

They looked at it closely. The stunned bird lay very still.

"Is it hurt? Does it need first aid?" Nora asked.

Dad said, "It's just scared. It needs to rest. We should be able to help."

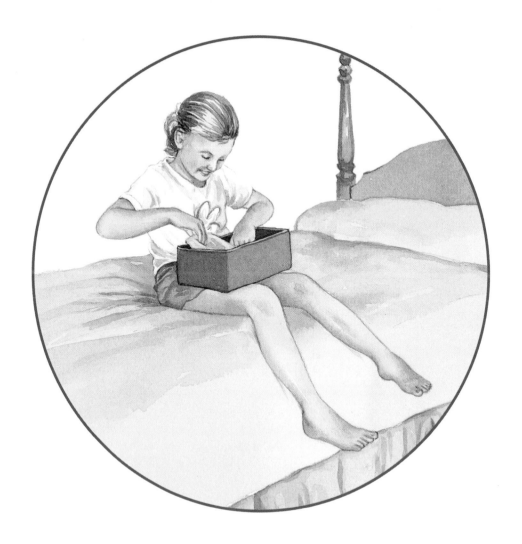

Nora ran to get a box to make a bed for the baby bird. She put a soft cloth in it. Dad picked up the bird gently. It looked so small in Dad's hand! It hardly weighed an ounce. Dad put it in the box.

"Should we get a cage?" asked Nora.

"No," replied Dad. "It will be all right. Let's just wait a while. Once it wakes up, it should be able to return to its home," Dad whispered.

Later Dad and Nora stood outside. They stayed away from the box. They didn't want to disturb the little bird.

"Good-bye, baby bird!" Nora cried. They watched the bird fly off. It landed on a branch in a nearby tree. Then it flew toward the sky.

Nora and Dad looked at each other. They smiled.

Wildlife Homes in the City

by Art Brown

Many people don't think that wildlife can be found in the city. This is untrue. Wildlife is any animal life that is not a pet being cared for in the home of a person. Cities are crawling with many kinds of wildlife in many different places.

Sidewalks

Sidewalks are homes to ants, beetles, and earthworms. You may not always see them on the sidewalk, though. They are often out only in predawn hours. When the sidewalks get too hot from the day's sun, they are unfit for this kind of wildlife. These crawlers hide underneath to keep cool.

Railroad Tracks

Railroad tracks are where snakes, lizards, and rabbits make their homes in the city. The gravel beside the tracks is a great place for snakes and lizards to lie in the sun. The quiet banks near the tracks are a peaceful place for rabbits to raise their young.

Empty Lots

Empty lots are deserted pieces of land. Different families of animals find food and homes in these lots at different times. Winged wildlife, such as butterflies and birds, are the first to show up for a brief stay. Crawlers and hoppers—centipedes and grasshoppers—follow them. Later small rodents, such as rats, make their homes among this wasted land.

Tall Buildings

Tall buildings in the city are like cliffs to many birds. Feathered wildlife such as pigeons, hawks, and falcons look toward the sky for a place to roost and nest. The high perches of tall buildings are a great place to watch for prey below.

Next time you are in the city, pay close attention to the sounds you hear and the life you see. There are many wildlife homes for you to find in the city. Prepare yourself for a treat. Look up and look down.

Night Life

by Sally Lee

It is dark outside. You are going to bed. But some animals are just getting up. They are hungry after sleeping all day. They like to hunt for food at night. They feel safer in the dark. Come visit their secret world.

What are those things flying through the air? They are not birds, so they must be bats.

Bats can't see in the dark. But they don't run into things. They have a clever way of getting around. They make a tiny noise while they fly. The noise is so high we can't hear it. The noise bounces off things around them. The bats hear the noise when it bounces back. Then they know where everything is. This is how bats find their food.

A little mouse runs through the grass. It can't see very well. But it knows its way around. The mouse uses its nose to smell the air. The smells tell the mouse where food is.

Watch out, little mouse! Someone wants to eat you for breakfast!

An owl sits on the branch of a tree. It has big eyes to help it see at night. But it does not need its big eyes to find the mouse. The owl can hear even tiny noises. It hears the mouse running in the grass. The owl flies right to the mouse's hiding place. But the mouse gets back to its nest just in time.

A tree falls in the woods. But who would be cutting down trees at night? It must be the beaver family. They are building a new house.

The beavers use their strong teeth to cut off branches. They can even cut through the trunks of small trees. After a while, the tree falls. Then the beavers pull it to the pond. That is where they are building their house. They use mud to hold the branches in place.

Who is that funny animal with dark rings around its yellow eyes? Don't be frightened. It is only a raccoon. It smells the air and listens for sounds. It looks around the pond for something to eat.

Raccoons use their paws like little hands when they eat. They are very clean. They like to wash their food before they eat it.

All night long the animals hunt and eat and play in the dark. But now the sky is getting light. The sun is about to come up. All the night animals go home to sleep. But they will be back tomorrow night.

What Is It?

by Rosalie Koskimaki

illustrated by Steve Henry

"What is it?" Simone asked her father. She showed him the tiny egg she found. "I found it on one of the posies by the road," she said.

"We'll let it be a surprise," her father told her. "Ask Mom to loan you a jar. Then put the egg in the jar and wait."

So Simone waited.

One day a worm came out of the egg.

Simone ran to her father. "I know what it is," she told him. "It's a worm. That was a worm egg I found."

"Well, it could be a worm egg," said her father, "but you'd better wait some more. Put some leaves in the jar."

So Simone did, and she waited. And the worm grew.

Then one day she saw the worm hiding itself. It was all wrapped up in a white thing like a blanket. Soon she couldn't see the worm anymore.

"What is that white thing?" Simone asked her father.

"That's a cocoon," he said.

"Then that was a cocoon egg I found," said Simone.

"No, I don't think so," said Simone's father. "You wait a bit longer."

All I do is wait, Simone thought.

But one day she saw the cocoon moving.
Then something started coming out of the
cocoon. In a short time Simone could see a
beautiful butterfly. She watched it fly around
in the jar.

At last Simone knew what kind of egg she
had found!

"The caterpillar hatched from the egg," said
Simone's father. "Then it built the cocoon. The
cocoon is a special case. It protected the
caterpillar as it turned into a butterfly."

"I think I'll write a poem about my
butterfly," she said.

"I think that is a wonderful idea," replied
her father.

Mathew and the Squirrel

by Abby Merli

illustrated by Laura Jacobson

One sunny spring day, Mathew was sitting outside and putting on his new roller skates. Suddenly he heard a strange noise. It sounded like a tiny scream for help. He wondered what could be making the sound. Then, about three feet away, he saw a scared baby squirrel lying in the grass.

Mathew could see that the cute little squirrel needed help. It must have fallen from its nest! It was too small to climb back up the tree.

Mathew sprang to his feet. He ran straight
to the home of his neighbor, Mrs. Scott. Mrs.
Scott had a very special skill. She knew how
to take care of wild animals that were too
young to care for themselves. She also took
care of animals that had been hurt. She would
rescue the baby squirrel.

Mrs. Scott ran back to the squirrel with Mathew. She gently scooped up the little animal in a tissue. Then she put it into the box Mathew's skates had been in. At first it struggled to get out. Then it squirmed around making a little nest for itself in one corner. It didn't take long for the squirrel to get used to the box.

"Let's take it back to my house," said Mrs. Scott. "You can become my pupil. You can learn how to take care of babies like this one."

As usual at Mrs. Scott's house, Mathew was greeted by an animal concert. Animals squeaked and squawked. Cages, boxes, tanks, and tubs were scattered throughout the house. There were three baby chipmunks in one cage. In another was a striped skunk! A screech owl with a broken wing was sleeping in one corner of the room. There were few empty spots.

Mrs. Scott checked the little squirrel carefully. "This looks like a healthy little squirrel," she told Mathew. "After a week or two here, I think your squirrel will be ready to scamper off on its own."

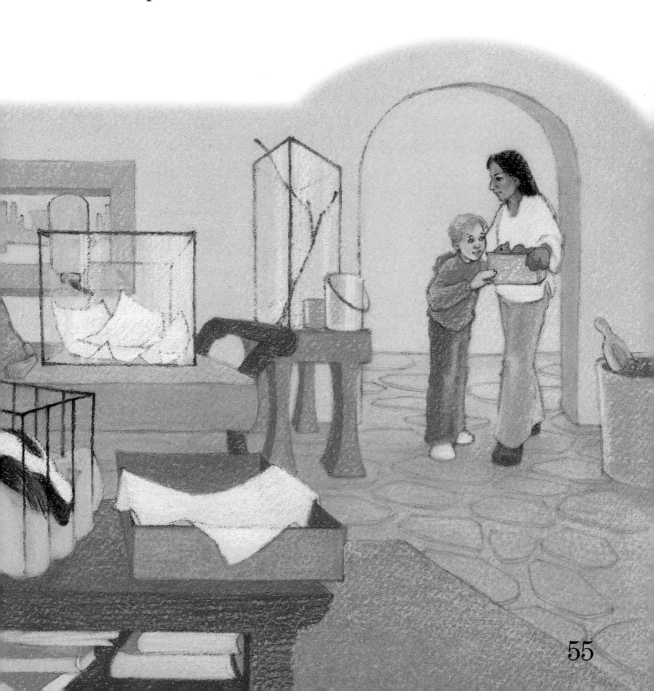

Language of the Bees

by Nina Smiley

When you know something wonderful, you want to share it. But what if you can't speak or write? You might try doing what bees do.

Bees talk. But their language has no words. Bees communicate with their bodies. Here's what they do.

On a warm April day, a worker bee travels far from the hive to find food. The food is called nectar. Nectar is a sweet substance that comes from flowers. The bee finds flowers. It busily goes from flower to flower to collect nectar. It eats some nectar and carries some home.

The bee feeds the nectar to other bees, but they want more. How can the bee tell them where it came from? It can't use words. So it uses its body. Bees communicate by dancing. The bee zigs and zags. It bobbles and wobbles. It flies in circles. This aerial dance tells the bees which way to go. It also reveals how far away the flowers are.

Soon the bees are on their way. They know
where the flowers are. The other bee told them.

Reading Reflections

These questions can help you think about the stories you have just read. After you write your responses, discuss them with a partner.

Focus on the Characters

- How are the bat, the mouse, and the owl alike in "Night Life"? How are they different?

- At the end of "Good-bye, Baby Bird," Nora and her father look at each other and smile. Why do they smile at one another?

- "Language of the Bees" explains how bees are able to communicate with their bodies. Why is it important for bees to communicate with each other?

Focus on the Stories

- In "What Is It?" Simone provides a temporary home for a cocoon. Name another story in this unit in which someone adopts a wild creature for a short while.

- Mrs. Scott in "Mathew and the Squirrel" is very patient, kind, and knowledgeable about animals. Name another character in this unit who is similar to Mrs. Scott.

- What was your favorite story in this unit? Explain your choice.

Focus on the Theme

- Name a selection from this unit that provides factual information about city wildlife.
- People must often come to the aid of injured wild animals. Name two stories in this unit in which the characters help a wild animal.
- Why do you think some people are surprised to find wildlife in the city?

The Clouds

by Abraham Stern
illustrated by Yvette Banek

The blue summer sky was filled with clouds.
Some were round. Others were flat. A few
were like big feather plumes. It was a beautiful
afternoon.

Patty and Sam were playing in the park.

"Let's play clouds," Patty said.

"How do you play?" Sam asked.

"First you look at a cloud," Patty said. "Then describe what it looks like."

63

"That cloud looks like an elephant," Sam said. "See the long nose?"

"That one has a big tail," Patty said. "It reminds me of a dinosaur."

Patty's little brother came from the sandbox.

64

"Do you see that big round cloud, Michael?" Patty asked.

"Yes," Michael said.

"Tell the truth. What does it look like?" Patty asked.

"You can't fool me," Michael said. "It looks just like a cloud."

Beatrix Potter's Rabbits

by Evan Owen
illustrated by Susan Spellman

Beatrix Potter stood at a window of her home in London, England. She watched two children walk by. The young girl wanted to play with them. But she didn't know them.

Beatrix was often alone. She had a brother, but he was away at school. And she did not see her parents very much. They were too busy. A nurse took care of her.

Each day was the same. Before lunch Beatrix played with her dolls. Later her nurse took her for a walk. Then they went back to the empty house.

Beatrix grew older. But she did not go away to school. A teacher came to her house. She rarely met other children.

One summer Beatrix was sent to the country. For the first time she saw live farm animals. She liked to watch the cows and sheep. She laughed at the pigs. But she loved the rabbits best of all.

Beatrix made some of these animals her pets. She gave them names. She drew pictures of them. She made up stories about them. In her stories the rabbits walked on two legs. They wore little coats. Some even wore hats. These rabbits were like real friends to her.

At the end of that summer Beatrix had to move back to London. But she never felt quite so lonely again. Now she had her animal friends to write about and to draw.

Years went by. Beatrix became a young woman. One of her teachers had a small boy. He was very ill, and he had to be in bed for a long time.

Beatrix was a thoughtful person. She knew how cheerless it is to be alone. So she wrote him letters. She told him stories about the rabbits. And she drew pictures to go with them.

The boy liked the stories. He showed them to his friends. They liked them too. So Beatrix Potter put the stories and pictures into a book. This book would earn her many admirers. Children all over the world have read it. Maybe you have too. It is called *The Tale of Peter Rabbit.*

Max and the Watchtower

by Margaret Young
illustrated by Dave Blanchette

There was nothing special about Max's town, except for the old fire watchtower in the middle of the fields near his house. No one went there to watch for fires anymore. But Max had a special fondness for the tower. He went there every day. That's where he went to lead his crew!

All around the tower were fields of soybeans as far as the eye could see. Every day after school, Max hurried home, did his homework, and raced out the door in excitement. He couldn't wait to get to the tower.

Max would climb the tower steps and take his station at the rail. On the tower, he was no longer a boy. He became Captain Max, sailing his trusty boat called the *Royal Blue*. There his crew of strong sailors, ready for their next adventure, joined him. They were looking for a sunken treasure of gold coins.

Max would look out across the sand and then study his map for the location of the gold. Then he would point his spyglass at the fields below, raise his voice, and steer his crew to riches. They would toil long and hard for their captain. They were loyal to him. They trusted his judgment. This gave Captain Max great joy.

It was almost dark when Max returned home to join his parents for dinner. They always knew where he had been. Every day they asked him the same questions.

"What did you do at that old tower today?" asked his mother.

"Anything new out there?" asked his father.

Max always smiled and replied, "Same old sea of plants as far as the eye can see." But they knew that he always saw much more! And they knew that tomorrow Max would be right back at the tower.

Pictures in Her Mind

by Lisa Yount

illustrated by Rosario Valderrama

Rosa lay still in her bed. The sun was bright.
But her room was dark. The doctor had said it
must be. "Your eyes must rest if you want
them to get well," he had told her.

Rosa had caught a serious illness. It had hurt her eyes. She knew they might not get well. She thought of that often, and each time she would cry. Rosa loved the beauty of the world.

No one else was in the house now. Her family had gone to the *fiesta*. Rosa could hear its glad sounds from far off. A new thought scared her. What if she forgot what a *fiesta* looked like?

She could not let that be. She would work on that right now.

Rosa thought hard. Soon she could see the *fiesta* in her mind. She saw the women's red-and-blue dresses. She saw the men's bright shirts. She saw the quick feet of the men and women as they danced.

She worked on the picture in her mind. It
became bright and clear. It was full of action
and color. She made sure she left nothing out.
When the picture was done, she felt calmer
and happier.

As the days passed, Rosa made more pictures in her mind. She thought of the way her mother's hands moved, quick and sure. She thought of the lines in her father's face. She worked to "see" each then as she had "seen" the *fiesta*.

At last Rosa's eyes got well. Now, when she looked at a thing, she looked with care. She stored the picture in her mind to keep.

Soon she began to put her pictures on paper. She worked at them until they were as clear as the ones in her mind. People liked her pictures. They liked seeing things the way Rosa saw them in her mind. "You should become an artist someday," they said. And you know what? She did!

What's Wrong with Make-Believe?

by Joshua Young
illustrated by Lane Gregory

Everything comes from someplace. Milk comes from cows. Wood comes from trees. Rain comes from clouds. Honey comes from bees.

Where does make-believe come from? It comes from you. It comes from your mind.

Make-believe is what you think up for yourself. Then you can act it out. You may use your body and your voice. You may play at being a prince. Or a pirate. Or an astronaut on the moon.

But make-believe isn't just for children!

Grown-ups enjoy make-believe too. They use it when they write stories. The library is filled with make-believe books. Grown-ups made up these stories. Then they put them in books. They used their imagination to create interesting stories. Now others can read them. The stories aren't true. The people in the stories never really lived. This kind of make-believe is called *fiction*.

You've seen make-believe in films. Who made the films? Grown-ups did, using their imaginations. Film stories tell about many things. Some are about soldiers or cowboys. Some are about ghosts or animals that talk. Some films seem very real. They may be about people like you. But they're still made up. Being made up doesn't spoil the story.

Grown-ups also paint make-believe pictures. Have you ever seen a strange picture? One that didn't look real? Maybe it showed a lady with a green face. Or a horse that was blue. Or houses floating in the air. Where did the painter see such things? The painter saw them in his or her mind. The painter imagined them and then painted them.

So what's wrong with making believe?
Nothing at all. Some people do it all their lives.
Will you?

The Astronaut

by Eloise Bradley Fink
illustrated by Larry Johnson

Sara couldn't sleep. Aunt Mae's house was too still—and dark. The clock's numbers flipped and the minutes glowed green. Sara watched them. They were like a rocket countdown turned around.

A small machine started up. It was only Simba, purring in cat dreams. Sara smiled. She closed her eyes.

    Her blanket was a cloud. She and Simba
floated up on it. Light as balloons, they flew
toward the stars.

    Sara piloted her cloud ship to a space
station. It glowed green like the clock—and
Simba's eyes. Sara parked in the structure. She
wrote a secret message. She poked it through
a window. Flip! It landed in a mail drop.

Like a kangaroo, Sara's ship leaped up.
Quick as a wink, it flew away. It flew toward
Earth, skipping stars. Sara wished she had a
photograph of the stars. The ship came down
silvery smooth, like a waterfall. The sun was
a giant orange in the trees.

"Wake up, Sara," exclaimed her aunt.
"I brought your orange juice, dear."
Sara smiled. "Mmmm, thanks. It's sunshine
in a glass."

Reading Reflections

These questions can help you think about the stories you have just read. After you write your responses, discuss them with a partner.

Focus on the Characters

- How is Patty's view of the clouds different from her brother's in "The Clouds"?
- In "Pictures in Her Mind" why is it so important for Rosa to create pictures in her mind?
- Imagine that Max from "Max and the Watchtower" and Patty and Sam from "The Clouds" become friends. Do you think Max would enjoy playing clouds with Patty and Sam? Why or why not?

Focus on the Stories

- In "Max and the Watchtower" Max uses his imagination to become a captain who travels across the sea. Name another story in this unit in which traveling to another place is the result of imaginative thinking.
- Imagination allows people to create make-believe friendships. Beatrix Potter often pretended that the rabbits on a farm

were her friends. Name another story in which a person creates a make-believe friendship.

- After reading "What's Wrong with Make-Believe?" who do you think uses imagination more often—grown-ups or children? Explain your choice.

Focus on the Theme

- People use make-believe for different reasons. Name a story from this unit in which the characters use make-believe to entertain themselves. Then name a story about a person who uses make-believe to cure loneliness.
- "What's Wrong with Make-Believe?" shares ways that grown-ups use imagination in their work. Name another story in which an adult uses his or her imagination to share creative talents with others.
- Do you like to pretend? Share a favorite way you have used your imagination to make-believe.

The Fish Princess

by Teresa Castillo
illustrated by Pat Paris

A king lived in a castle by the sea. His daughter loved him dearly. She enjoyed telling him stories. She also adored the sea. Each day she swam for almost eight hours.

This made the king angry. "The princess always swims! She shouldn't look wet!" he roared. "She wears gold rings. She tells stories. She laughs and sings. She sits and sews. She doesn't act like a fish!"

The princess tried to explain. But the king wouldn't listen. "Promise me you'll stop all this swimming," he said.

"I can't promise that," she said.

So the king locked her in the tower. "You'll stay here until you can!"

"I wish I *were* a fish," the sad princess cried. In a flash, she became a fish. She leaped from the tower. She splashed into the sea and swam away. She felt liberated.

Days passed, then weeks. The king was worried. His daughter was gone. One day he went walking. "How wrong I was," he sighed. "I should have let her be herself."

A fish was nearby. It heard the king. Splash! It changed back into the princess. She told the king many stories about being a fish. And the king and the princess were happy ever after.

The Storyteller

by Rosalie Koskimaki
illustrated by Susan Spellman

Hans Christian Andersen was born long ago in Denmark. His parents were very poor. His father made shoes. He didn't sell many, so there wasn't much money.

Hans often felt blue. And he wasn't very strong. Other children laughed at him, so he usually didn't play with them. He had few friends. Instead, he made up stories. He got his fun from make-believe. When he was eleven, his father died.

As Hans grew up, things got a little better. He wrote some books. They were for grown-ups. But then he thought about his boyhood.

"I was a sad little boy," said Hans. "Children shouldn't be sad. I will make up some stories for children. The stories will make them happy."

So Hans wrote four stories for children. They were "The Tinder Box," "Little Claus and Big Claus," "Little Ida's Flowers," and "The Princess and the Pea."

Children loved the stories. Even grown-ups liked them. Hans became very famous, and he wrote more stories. He wrote "Thumbelina," "The Emperor's New Clothes," "The Ugly Duckling," and "The Tin Soldier." After that he continued to write many more.

Many children have read these stories. Hans
Christian Andersen did what he said he would
do. He made up stories to make children
happy. Maybe you'll read one aloud to
someone and make him or her feel happy, too.

Tall Tales

by David Carver

Stories can be told in many ways. They can be written down. They can be told aloud. They can be shown through pictures. Did you know that sometimes these pictures are carved on trees, too?

The Native Americans along the Pacific Coast had no written words. So they carved their stories on trees. These trees are called totem poles.

Making a Totem Pole

Here's how they made totem poles. First they cut down a tree. Using tools, artists carved figures all along the trunk of the tree. The artist with the best imagination carved the most important figures. The figures might be animals, like frogs or foxes. Or they might be carvings of the sun and the moon, or the chief or his daughter. Together these carvings told a story.

The Totem Pole Story

The totem pole was like a family album on a tree. It might tell if the family had a lot of money or power. The totem pole could tell about brothers and sisters. It could show aunts and uncles. If an uncle was a good fisher, the artist might carve a picture of a salmon. If he was brave, you might see the face of a bear.

Finishing the Totem Pole

The totem pole was sometimes painted. Then it was lifted so it stood up straight. Some totem poles are still standing after 100 years.

The most important carvings were usually at the bottom. That's because the poles were so tall that it was hard to see their tops. Some totem poles were 60 feet tall or taller. That's as high as twelve children standing on each other's shoulders!

The next time you see a picture of a totem pole, look at it carefully. Use the carvings to read a story about the life of a Native American family.

Dark House

by Pamela Bliss

illustrated by Janice Skivington

It was sundown, and a strong wind roared outside. Dwight and Ricky were listening to music. All at once, the lights went out!

"Oh, no!" Dwight cried. "The power went off! What do we do now?"

"Now we can have some real fun. I can't wait!" Grandpa said.

"How?" Ricky asked. "We can't listen to music or work on our puzzle."

"I know how," smiled Mother. She got eight candles out of the cupboard.

Father lit the stove. He handed Mother
some matches. Then he made popcorn in a
pan for everyone. *Pop! Pop!*

"Let's all get in a circle," Grandpa said.
Dwight and Ricky sat on the floor. They were
curious. What would happen next?

"Once upon a time, there was a giant
jackal . . ." Grandpa started.

"This is neat," Dwight whispered to Ricky.
"The room is dark as night. This is like story
time at summer camp."

The World's Best-Known Story

by Katie Hahn
illustrated by Yvonne Gilbert

Do you know which is the most famous story in the world? It's one you've probably known since you were very small. It's been told all over the world. You can find it in books, plays, films, and on television. It is "Cinderella."

"Cinderella" has been told in many different ways. Parts of it may be changed. But the main story is always the same. A rich boy meets a poor girl who is nice and kind. They fall in love, but the boy loses the girl. Then he finds her again. They live happily ever after.

One version of "Cinderella" was written by the Grimm brothers. They were German writers. They heard fairy tales from many people. The Grimms decided to collect the tales in one book. It was printed in 1812. "Cinderella" was in it.

As the Grimms tell the story, Cinderella's life is hard. Her father is too firm with her. But special birds help her. She goes to the dance. She meets the young man. Then she loses her fur shoe.

The most famous "Cinderella" was written in 1697. Its author was French. Like the Grimms, he used old folktales he had heard. But he did something the Grimms didn't do. He changed the style of the tales to suit his readers. He wrote for rich people. They lived with the French king. Their lives were filled with comfort. They knew about coaches and what servants were.

For these readers, he wrote a sweet Cinderella story. He took out the cruelty that was in many of the folktales. Instead, he put in some humor. The pumpkin that becomes a coach was his idea. Cinderella's glass slipper was his idea, too.

After all these years, the tale of Cinderella is still told. And it is still loved just as much. We all like happy endings. We're glad Cinderella finds love after all her problems.

Today, you may hear someone talk about "a Cinderella story." This means any tale in which a poor but good person is rewarded at last. The reward may be love, money, or happiness.

The Story-Quilt Artist

by Chris Meramec

Faith Ringgold is an artist who creates special works of art. Some artists make paintings. Faith has made paintings, too. But much of Faith's art is made from cloth. She uses fabrics and paints to make quilts that tell stories.

When Faith Ringgold was a little girl, she had asthma. Many days, she was too sick to go to school. Faith's mother took care of her. She helped Faith do her schoolwork. She did not want Faith to fall behind.

When Faith finished her schoolwork, her mother gave her crayons and paper. She also gave Faith pieces of cloth, needles, and thread. She urged Faith to create whatever she wanted.

Faith (far right) with her brother and sister

Faith went to college and studied to be an art teacher. She taught in New York City public schools for twenty years. She worked on her paintings in her spare time.

Later, Faith taught art to college students. She had students use things such as cloth and beads to make art. One day, a student saw some of Faith's paintings. The student wondered why Faith didn't use cloth in her own art.

Working with cloth was a tradition in Faith's family. Her mother made dresses. Her grandmothers made quilts. Faith remembered the scraps of cloth her mother gave her as a child. She began trying to make art with cloth. She quit teaching. She started working full time on her art. She made masks. Then she made cloth sculptures.

Faith also started making quilts. Quilts have many pieces. The pieces are sewed together to make pictures. Faith's quilts have many pictures. Many of Faith's quilts tell stories. She calls them story quilts.

One story quilt is called *Tar Beach*. It shows a family in Harlem. In the summer, the family sits on the roof of their building. The adults talk while the children sleep. The story of the quilt is written around the edge. The story quilt was even made into a book called *Tar Beach*. The book has pleased many people and won many awards. It is in an art museum.

In her art, Faith shows objects and experiences in different ways. She also shows how pictures can tell a story, even on quilts.

Reading Reflections

These questions can help you think about the stories you have just read. After you write your responses, discuss them with a partner.

Focus on the Characters

- What lesson does the king learn in "The Fish Princess"?
- Think of two adjectives that describe Hans Christian Andersen in "The Storyteller." Explain your choices.
- Which version of "Cinderella" in "The World's Best-Known Story" do you like the most? Why?

Focus on the Stories

- "The Storyteller" provides details about real-life writer Hans Christian Andersen. Name another selection in this unit that is a biography of a storyteller.
- "The Story-Quilt Artist" shows how a storyteller may use pictures to tell a story. Name another story in this unit in which pictures tell a story.
- How are "The Fish Princess" and the story of Cinderella alike? How are they different?

Focus on the Theme

- Hans Christian Andersen wrote stories to make children feel happy. What stories in this unit have happy endings?

- If you were asked to create a totem pole to tell your family's history, what symbols would you include?

- This unit tells about the different ways stories are shared. Stories may be told using words, either written or spoken. Pictures are also often used to tell stories. Do you prefer to hear, read, or look at stories? Explain your choice.

Using Your Cents

by David Grahm
illustrated by Lane Gregory

It was Cindy's birthday. As usual, her grandparents gave her some birthday money. "Buy yourself something special," they told her.

Cindy never had trouble deciding how to spend the money. She always went to Al's Toy Store, a store with a large selection of toys. She would look over Al's collection of stuffed animals. It included bears, monkeys, sheep, birds, fish, and more. Some were big, and some were babies. Each year, Cindy would buy the one or two animals she liked most.

This year was different, however. Cindy entered the store and looked at the shelves. But, she could not find any animals she really liked.

127

At last she thought, "I guess the little red foxes look okay, and so do the babies." She used her last pennies to pay for them.

At home, Cindy added the foxes to the rest of her collection, but she played with them very little.

Several months later, Cindy was strolling by Al's Toy Store. In the window she saw some new stuffed animals on sale, including baby goats, deer, and mice.

"Now, those babies are really cute!" Cindy thought. "But I have no money to pay for them. Maybe I can make a trade."

She entered the store and talked to Al.

"Sorry, Cindy," Al said, "but you bought the foxes a long time ago. I can't let you trade them now for the newer animals."

Later, Cindy told her parents her problem.
"Let this be a lesson," her father said. "When
you have money, you don't have to spend it all
right away. To avoid misfortune, save it until
you are sure of what you want to buy. That
makes good sense!"

Carmen's Penny

by Albert Bartlett
illustrated by Beatriz Rodriguez

Elsa's dad was folding clothes. He asked
Elsa to go to the store for him. He gave her a
list and some money. As Elsa was leaving,
Carmen ran up to her. She begged to join Elsa.
Elsa had planned to ride her bike, but she
couldn't if Carmen was tagging along. Since
Carmen loved to go to the store, Elsa agreed
to take her.

Elsa muttered all the way to the store about not being able to ride her bike. Carmen asked Elsa to give her a piggyback ride. Elsa replied unkindly, "No, you wanted to come along, so you can just walk." They walked the rest of the way in silence.

At the store the girls gathered all of the items on the list. They stood in the checkout line for a long time because the store was quite busy. Finally, their turn came. When Elsa saw the total she nearly panicked. It was three cents more than she had! Elsa was worried. Her mind started racing. She tried to think of a solution to her problem. She checked all of her pockets twice. When she didn't find any more money, she told the clerk, "I'm sorry, but I don't have enough money. Could we put something back on the shelf?"

Just then Carmen reached into her pocket and calmly pulled out a coin. "Do you want this penny?" Carmen asked Elsa, holding a nickel out to her. Elsa glanced down at the money. She smiled in relief, pleased. Then she handed the money to the clerk.

After the girls left the store, Elsa gave Carmen a big hug. Elsa said, "Do you know you saved the day? You're a whiz! Dad will be so proud when I tell him how you helped me out. How would you like it if we spent some time doing what you want to do?"

The Dog Wash

by Carol Mrozinski

illustrated by Janice Skivington

Sam and his friends were at the school playground early one Saturday morning. They had a hose, some tubs of water, soap, and plenty of towels. They put up a big sign with the phrase "Dog Wash Today."

Then they waited. They waited and waited. Many people walked past, but no one brought a dog. "Oh, no," said Paco, stretching. "I knew this was a terrible idea. Now we won't be able to go to Sports Day."

But just then a man and two girls arrived with their dogs. They brought three lovable dogs to wash. Paco, Al, and Linda began to wash the man's dogs. Sam and Tasha began to wash the girls' dog. Soon more dogs arrived. All the students in Sam's class were busy. Some were scrubbing dogs, and others were drying them. Maria was busy selling tickets to more dog owners.

Everything went well when suddenly a fire truck streaked past. Its siren screeched slowly and shrilly. Dogs burst into howls. One wet, soapy dog jumped out of its tub and began running around the playground. Others began to chase it. Soon dogs were running in all directions. Kids and owners were racing after them. When they finally caught all the dogs, the kids washed and dried them. Sam said, "I think I'll vote for a car wash next time!"

Funny Money

by Amy Lawless
illustrated by Pat Paris

Long ago, people didn't go to an office or factory to earn money. They found it on the ground. The money was large, round, and flat. It looked just like what it was—a stone!

Because the stones were special and very hard to find, they were valuable. The larger the stone, the more it was worth. The smallest money stone—about the size of a dinner plate—might buy a few fish or a small pig.

Slaves carried the big stones when people went shopping. The richest men had stones too big and heavy to carry around. The men left these stones in front of their houses. Everyone could see how rich they were.

Some people found their money at the seashore. They used red, black, and white shells. The women broke the shells into small fragments. They polished them carefully and made holes in them. Then they strung the pieces on strings. One string of shell money would buy food. A hundred strings might buy a small boat or a cow.

Some people could eat their money. They made money out of salt. They shaped it into small bricks. The bricks were all of the same size and value. They were stamped with a picture of the king. This means the king would accept salt as money. If the king would take it, then everyone else would too.

Salt money wasn't as heavy as stone money. It wasn't as hard to find as shell money. But when it rained, salt money might melt.

Finally people started using metal for money. They used copper and silver and gold. Metal wasn't easily hurt by water or heat or time. And since there wasn't very much of it, everyone wanted it. Metal money was made in many shapes. It was made in chunks, circles, and rings. Some of it was shaped and stamped like salt money.

Metal money is much better than salt or shell or stone money. But if you have a lot of it, metal money is hard to carry around. It is heavy and takes up too much space. So today we also have paper money. It has numbers printed on it to show how much the money is worth.

Heather's Quarters

by George Sibberson
illustrated by Deborah J. White

"Hi, Heather!" Mr. Taylor said as Heather
entered the store. "What can I do for you today?"
"I have two quarters to spend. I'd like to look
around awhile before I decide," Heather said.

"Take your time," Mr. Taylor said. Heather was walking by the comic books when she bumped into a rack of birthday cards. She dropped one of her quarters. As she stooped to look for it, she heard another coin drop. A man wearing a green sweatshirt kneeled near her. He looked under a toy shelf.

Just as Heather spied her quarter beneath the shelf, the man snatched it. He thought it was his. The man dropped the quarter into his pocket and left.

Upset and disappointed, Heather began searching again. Suddenly, a flash of gold caught her eye. "Look, Mr. Taylor! I'll bet this belongs to the man who found my quarter," she said as she held up a shiny coin.

Mr. Taylor looked at the coin. He said in surprise, "That's a twenty-dollar gold piece!"

Just then the door flew open. The man in the green sweatshirt burst in. "I've lost my lucky gold piece!" he shouted.

"This little girl just found an unusual coin," Mr. Taylor said, pointing to the coin in Heather's hand. "Perhaps she'd trade it for the quarter you found."

"Make it two quarters!" the man offered quickly and he dropped two quarters into Heather's palm. "I'm sorry. It's my fault. I didn't notice which coin I'd dropped when I picked up your quarter. Thank you so much. I've had that lucky gold piece for years."

Heather jingled her three coins. She grinned from ear to ear. "Mr. Taylor," she chuckled, "I think it'll take me even longer to make up my mind now."

The Peddler of Swaffham

by Peter Churchill
illustrated by Yvonne Gilbert

One night as John Chapman lay in bed, he had a strange dream. He dreamed he heard a voice.

"John!" called the voice. "Would you like to be rich?"

"Of course," said John, still asleep.

"Then go to London," said the voice. "Wait on the bridge. There you'll find your fortune."

The next day John set out for London. He wore his best hat with a feather in it. London was a long way from Swaffham, where he lived. But he didn't mind. He was a peddler by trade, and used to walking. Besides, he had his dog with him for company.

When he got to London he waited on the bridge. Soon a man came up to him. "What are you doing?" he asked.

"I'm looking for my fortune," said John.

"Well," explained the man, "if I were you, I wouldn't wait here. I'd go straight to a place called Swaffham. A peddler lives there. In his garden there is a pear tree. I had a dream about that tree one day. A lot of gold was lying under it. I suppose I could go and dig it up myself. But I don't believe in dreams. Good luck!"

John could not get home fast enough. He cut across the city and flew back to Swaffham. As soon as he was back, he started to dig in his very own garden. He found not one pot of gold, but two. He was rich for life!

In Swaffham today you can see a large wooden sign. It has a picture of John Chapman with his dog. And it says:

"The peddler of Swaffham who did by a dream find a great treasure."

Reading Reflections

These questions can help you think about the stories you have just read. After you write your responses, discuss them with a partner.

Focus on the Characters

- What does Elsa think of Carmen at the beginning of "Carmen's Penny"? How does her attitude change by the end of the story?
- "Funny Money" describes the development of money over time. What advantages are there to using metal and paper money rather than using salt and stone?
- Do you think the characters in "The Dog Wash" will plan to earn money by washing dogs again? Why or why not?

Focus on the Stories

- Both Cindy in "Using Your Cents" and Heather in "Heather's Quarters" use their money to go shopping. How do they spend their money differently?
- In "Heather's Quarters" Heather receives more money unexpectedly when she trades the gold piece for her lost quarter. Name

another story from this unit in which a character receives money unexpectedly.

- A character's decisions can greatly change the outcome of a story. How would "The Peddler of Swaffham" have ended differently if the man in London had followed the advice of his dream?

Focus on the Theme

- Money, even a small coin, plays an important role in the stories in this unit. Name a story in which a single coin has great importance. Explain why it is so important.
- This unit shares many lessons about money. Cindy from "Using Your Cents" learns to spend her money more wisely. What lesson does Heather learn in "Heather's Quarters"? What lesson does the peddler learn in "The Peddler of Swaffham"?
- After reading this unit, what are some ways you can "use your cents" more wisely?

The Story of Wilbur and Charlotte

based on *Charlotte's Web* by E. B. White
adapted by Sasha Henry
illustrated by Barbara Kiwak

    At first, Wilbur didn't care much for spiders. But then he discovered how clever they were. He discovered what good friends they could be too.

    Wilbur was the runt of the mother pig's litter. All the other piglets were much bigger than he was. He was so tiny that the farmer was planning to kill him. You see, runts often don't grow up to be healthy animals. But Fern, the farmer's little girl, rescued Wilbur. She promised to take care of him.

Fern treated Wilbur like a baby. She fed
Wilbur milk from a baby bottle. She gave him
rides in her doll's carriage. She played with
him and loved him. When Fern and her
brother went swimming, she took Wilbur
along. He played in the sticky mud beside the
brook. He liked that.

One day Fern's father said Wilbur was big
enough to sell. Fern hated to give Wilbur up,
but she had to sell him to her uncle. At least
she could visit him at her uncle's barn.

Fern loved the barn. It was big and old, and
it smelled good. But her uncle wouldn't let her
play with Wilbur. She could only sit and watch
him.

Wilbur was very lonely. The lamb wouldn't play with him. Neither would the bird. One rainy day Wilbur felt so sad, he just cried. He wanted a friend.

Then he heard a tiny voice. "I will be your friend," it said. The voice belonged to Charlotte, a gray spider.

Wilbur thought that Charlotte was pretty, although he was sad that she ate flies and bugs. He thought that was cruel. But he was happy to have a friend.

The summer days were lovely. Wilbur grew
to like Charlotte better all the time. He learned
that she helped everyone by getting rid of
flies. Nobody liked *them*. Wilbur didn't like
them either.

Meanwhile, Wilbur was growing bigger. He
ate three good meals every day. And he was a
happy pig.

Then one day the oldest sheep paid him a
visit. She commented about his size. Wilbur
answered that gaining weight was good for a
pig his age.

But the old sheep smiled. "These people are fattening you up, Wilbur," she said. "They're going to butcher you. By Christmas you'll be pork chops and bacon and ham."

Wilbur burst into tears. "I don't want to die," he cried. "I want to stay with my friends."

Charlotte had heard everything. "Wilbur," she said, "stop crying. You won't die. I'll save you."

And Charlotte began to think of a plan to save Wilbur.

The Rooster's Escape

based on "The Nun's Priest's Tale" from
The Canterbury Tales by Geoffrey Chaucer
adapted by Hannah Chandler
illustrated by Fabricio Vanden Broeck

An old woman lived on a farm with her two daughters. Among her farm animals was a rooster named Sir Chanticleer. How this rooster did crow! His voice was merry and strong.

Chanticleer lived in the barnyard with a hen named Dame Pertelote. One morning Chanticleer woke up shaking. He informed Pertelote, "I dreamed about a strange animal. It looked something like a dog. It was red, but its tail and ears had black tips. And it tried to eat me up!"

"Silly thing," interrupted Pertelote, "don't be afraid of a dream! Dreams come from overeating. I'll find you some special grasses to eat. They'll make these dreams go away!"

"Thank you," said Chanticleer, "but I think you're wrong. Dreams can come true! Many wise folk say so. Indeed, I heard about two sailors who planned a sea voyage. The night before sailing, one dreamed of drowning and refused to go. His friend went ahead, though. A storm wrecked the ship, and he drowned!"

165

Well, time passed, and soon it was spring. Chanticleer crowed happily. The hens napped in the warm sun, and all was well.

But not for long! Russell, a red fox, came into the yard. Chanticleer began to shake when he saw the animal from his dream! He started to run, but Russell spoke sweetly.

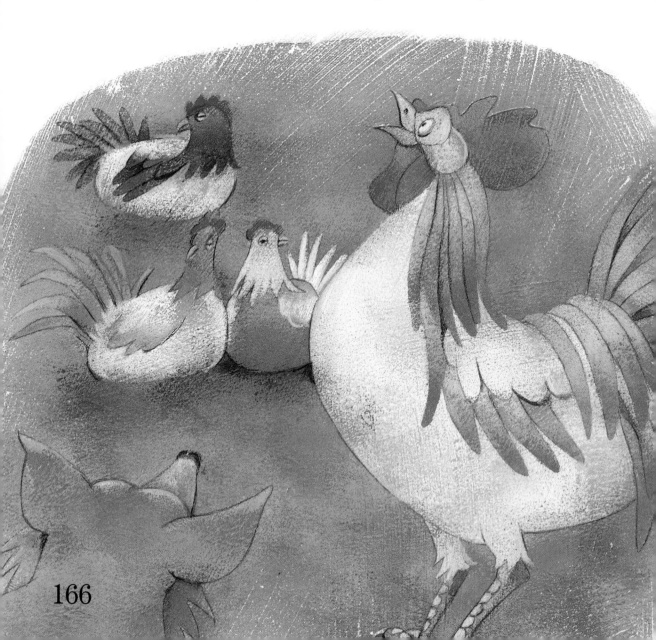

"Don't be afraid. I came here to listen to
your fine voice! Why, it's almost as good as
your father's was. Do you know why his was
so fine? He always closed his eyes and
stretched out his neck when he crowed. Try it
that way. I'm sure you'll sound as good."

Chanticleer's good sense left him. He shut his
eyes and stretched his neck. The fox grabbed
him by the throat and ran for the woods.

The hens woke up. The old woman heard
their squawks and, with her daughters, gave
chase. Neighbors and animals followed.

Caught in the fox's jaws, Chanticleer had a
novel idea. "You've outsmarted them!" he said.
"They'll never catch you. Why don't you tell
them to give up?"

"Good idea!" said Russell. But when he
opened his mouth, Chanticleer sprang free and
flew up into a tree.

168

"I was only having fun with you," said Russell. "It's a game. Come down and I'll tell you how it's played."

But Chanticleer wouldn't budge. "You can trick me once," he said, "but not twice."

Now I've *been tricked*, thought the fox. *I should have kept quiet. My dinner got away because I wanted to brag.*

So each one learned a lesson. Chanticleer learned not to believe everything he was told. Russell learned not to brag.

In their barnyard chats, Pertelote still says dreams are nonsense. But Chanticleer isn't so sure.

Tomcat

by Marguerite Dolch
illustrated by Jane Wright

Tomcat was a kind of wild cat. He'd lost bits of ears and fur in fights. One eye was almost closed from a scar. But he was a good hunter.

Tomcat lived in the Lees' barn. He caught rats and mice. The Lees milked their cows morning and night. Each day they left a bowl of milk in the barn for Tomcat.

Tomcat would wait until no one was around. Then he would drink the milk. No one had ever petted him. And I think no one had ever heard him purr.

Mrs. Lee's sister lived on a farm about an hour's walk from the Lees'. One day the sister brought her pet cat Molly to the Lees' house.

"I have to go away for three weeks," said Mrs. Lee's sister. "And Molly is going to have kittens shortly."

"I'll take care of Molly," Mrs. Lee told her. "I'll give her a box in the kitchen for her family."

But Molly didn't like the box in the kitchen. She went out to the barn. She made herself a nest in the hay. There she met Tomcat.

Molly loved Tomcat as soon as she saw him. She rubbed against him and purred. Tomcat caught mice and brought them to Molly. And Mr. Lee left two bowls of milk in the barn.

In two days Molly's kittens were born.
Tomcat sat next to the nest. He watched over
Molly all the time.

At the end of a week Molly let the Lees see that she had three kittens. Mrs. Lee carried them to the box in the kitchen. But Molly didn't like that. One by one she took her kittens back to her nest in the hay.

When the kittens were three weeks old, Mrs. Lee took all four cats back to her sister's farm.

Molly stayed at the farm just one night.

174

The next day Mrs. Lee saw Molly coming down the road. Molly had a kitten in her mouth. She seemed to be very tired. Mrs. Lee watched. Molly took the kitten to the barn. Then Molly and Tomcat came out of the barn. They walked down the road together.

The next morning Mr. Lee went to the barn to milk the cows. He saw Molly and Tomcat walking toward the barn. Each cat was carrying a kitten in its mouth. The two cats were very tired. All night long they had been walking. They carried the kittens to the barn and put them in the nest.

Mrs. Lee's sister felt it was wrong to take Molly away from Tomcat again. She waited until the kittens were bigger and then took them home.

And every day the Lees left two bowls of milk in the barn.

The Bravest Sheepdog

by Amelia La Croix
illustrated by Tom Barrett

David sat outside in the meadow, watching the sheep. It seemed like the hottest day of the year. Even sitting under a large tree, David found the heat very hard to take.

David wasn't alone with the flock. Shep, the family sheepdog, helped him. Shep was the gentlest, friendliest, and smartest dog that David had ever known. David smiled as he watched Shep run around the meadow. Shep saw to it that none of the sheep ran away.

David counted and then recounted the sheep to make sure they were all there. Neighbors had sent recent warnings of sheep attacks. This meant wolves were in the area.

As the time passed, David grew hotter. He wondered how the sheep could stand the hot sunshine. He decided to go inside the house for a while to cool off.

Inside, David lay down on the couch and soon fell asleep. Meanwhile, in the meadow, strangers were approaching through the bushes. Two wolves quietly made their way to the fence around the yard. They appeared, briefly disappeared in the bushes, and then reappeared. They leaped over the fence and slowly approached the flock.

Shep saw the wolves and began barking loudly. Bravely he stood between the sheep and the wolves, refusing to take one step back. He wondered why David wasn't outside.

The wolves inched closer, but Shep stood his ground. As he barked fiercely, the house door suddenly opened, and David hurried out. The wolves turned and quickly ran away.

"Why, Shep!" David cried. "You're not just the gentlest, friendliest, and smartest sheepdog ever. You're also the bravest!"

The Biggest Mouse in the World

by Charles House
illustrated by Gary Torrisi

Jimmy was a meadow mouse. He had wonderful ears.

He could hear the breezes when they whispered through the tall grass—*feeeeoooooo.*

He could hear an acorn fall out of an oak tree far away—*kuk.*

He could hear a snowflake when it nestled onto the soil next to his ear—*thuth.*

The reason Jimmy could hear so well was that he listened. He listened all the time. Jimmy was wise to listen. He couldn't see as well as other meadow mice. Perhaps he needed glasses.

One day Jimmy was looking for the tiny seeds he liked to eat for lunch. In the sky the great hawk could see Jimmy in the meadow. He dropped out of the sky like a falling star.

At the last second, Jimmy heard the wind whistling through the hawk's wings—*sssssss*. Jimmy scurried under a fallen tree trunk.

On another day the old owl saw Jimmy as he moved through the grass. The old owl flew swiftly and quietly toward Jimmy. Jimmy heard the air slip through the owl's wings—*phhhhhhhhhhhh*. Jimmy ran under a crooked old rock.

On another day the prowling fox crept toward Jimmy. He crouched down and got ready to leap. But Jimmy heard a *tst* as the fox's claws touched a stone. He ran into a hole in the ground and was safe.

One day Jimmy came to a place where there was a circle of very large seeds. They looked so good and so big!

Jimmy tried to eat one of the big seeds. But before he could reach it, his nose bumped into something hard.

He tried to eat another one of the big seeds. Again his nose bumped into something hard.

That something hard that Jimmy had found was a round piece of glass.

He used his paws to see if he could raise an edge of the circle of glass. He could. He looked beneath it and saw that the seeds were tiny. He set the glass down again and looked. The seeds were big!

What a wonderful thing! The glass made the small seeds turn big!

Then Jimmy lifted the whole glass off the ground. He found that if he walked on his hind legs he could carry the glass over his head with both paws. Jimmy was sure that now he would find seeds easily when he looked for his lunch.

Jimmy walked along carrying the circle of glass over his head. He was so happy about his great discovery! But he forgot to listen.

High in the air, the great hawk saw Jimmy. He dropped out of the sky like a falling star. At the very last second Jimmy heard the sound of the wind through feathers—*sssssss*.

Jimmy looked up through the circle of glass. He was frightened. What a huge, terrible hawk!

At the same time, the hawk looked through the glass at Jimmy. He spread his wings and slowed down—fast! Then he flew far away. The hawk was filled with fear. What a huge, terrible mouse! It was the biggest mouse in the world!

Now Jimmy always carries the circle of glass with him wherever he goes. The hawk, the owl, and the fox have moved away. They moved to a field where the mice are not so terrible or so huge.

Jimmy still lives in the meadow. There the seeds are bigger and easier to find than they ever were before.

Blaze and
the Fire

by C. W. Anderson
illustrated by Linda Pierce

Billy was a boy who loved horses more than anything else in the world. He loved his own horse, Blaze, best of all.

Every day he and Blaze would go riding. One day Billy decided to ride along a little winding road that passed through some woods.

Billy and Blaze had gone quite a long way when Blaze suddenly stopped. Billy looked ahead and saw smoke coming out of a pile of brush at the side of the road.

As Billy looked, the smoke turned to fire. He knew that the fire had to be put out, or it would spread to the nearby pine trees. Then the whole countryside might burn.

Billy had to get help quickly. The nearest place to go for help was a large farm. The quickest way to get there was to cut across a big field. But there was a high stone wall between Billy and the field. Blaze would have to jump it. It was higher than anything he'd ever jumped, but Blaze seemed to understand that this was important. He jumped the high wall perfectly.

They went quickly across the field. But then, in the middle of the field, they came to a brook. There was no bridge over it and no time to look for a shallow place to cross.

"Come on, Blaze," called Billy.

Blaze made a tremendous leap. As they landed, the bank gave way under the horse's hind feet. For a moment Billy thought that he and Blaze would fall back into the brook, but Blaze scrambled up the bank. In a flash they were off as fast as the horse could go.

193

Suddenly Billy pulled Blaze to a stop. There, right in front of them, was a high wall with barbed wire at the top.

"Just one more jump, Blaze," Billy whispered.

They were almost over the wall when Blaze's hind legs caught on the wire. It seemed certain that the horse would fall. But with a great effort, he managed to stay on his feet.

Blaze galloped into the farmyard, and the farmer hurried over. Billy told him about the fire, and at once the farmer ran to get some fire-fighting tools. He put the tools in his car and drove off very fast. His wife telephoned people nearby to send all the help they could.

Then she noticed that Blaze's legs had been cut. She brought warm water and medicine and helped Billy clean and bandage the cuts. She assured him that they weren't deep cuts and would soon heal.

Billy and Blaze rested for a while. Then they started for home. On the way, they met several of the farmers who had gone to help fight the fire. The farmers said that they had been able to put out the fire before it did any real harm. They thanked Billy for what he had done.

One morning, eight weeks later, someone
rapped at the door of Billy's house. Billy's
mother asked him to go and see who was
there. It was one of the farmers who had
helped put out the fire. He held a big box that
had the words "For Billy and Blaze" on it.

Billy was very excited as he opened the box. Inside he found a beautiful bridle for Blaze and a pair of shiny riding boots for himself. The people of the countryside had bought these things to show Billy and Blaze how truly grateful they were.

Billy put on his new boots. Then he took the new bridle down to the stable to put it on Blaze. Then he climbed onto Blaze's back, and the two friends started happily off for their daily ride.

Reading Reflections

These questions can help you think about the stories you have just read. After you write your responses, discuss them with a partner.

Focus on the Characters

- In "The Story of Wilbur and Charlotte" what are some qualities that Wilbur admires in his friend Charlotte?
- In "Blaze and the Fire" Blaze is able to jump higher and farther than ever before. Why do you think he is able to do this?
- Which quality is most valuable to Jimmy in "The Biggest Mouse in the World"—his superb hearing and ability to listen or the protection he gets from using the magnifying glass? Explain your choice.

Focus on the Stories

- Charlotte in "The Story of Wilbur and Charlotte" helps her friend Wilbur. Name another story in this unit in which one animal helps another animal.
- Jimmy is able to trick the hawk by using his magnifying glass to appear bigger. Name

another story in which an animal escapes by tricking another animal.

- After reading "The Story of Wilbur and Charlotte" and "The Rooster's Escape," would you want to read the entire books on which these selections are based? Why or why not?

Focus on the Theme

- Animals and people often must work together in the country. Name a story in this unit in which an animal helps prevent something bad from happening to the farm land.

- Country life involves risky situations for animals and people that are different from the risks found in the city. In this unit what are some of the dangers facing animals or people who live in the country?

- Which story in this unit do you think is the best example of country life? Explain your choice.

Glossary

Pronunciation Key

a as in **at**	**o** as in **ox**	**ou** as in **out**	**ch** as in **chair**
ā as in **late**	**ō** as in **rose**	**u** as in **up**	**hw** as in **which**
â as in **care**	**ô** as in **bought** and **raw**	**ū** as in **use**	**ng** as in **ring**
ä as in **father**		**ûr** as in **turn**; **germ**, **learn**, **firm**, **work**	**sh** as in **shop**
e as in **set**	**oi** as in **coin**		**th** as in **thin**
ē as in **me**	**o͞o** as in **book**	**ə** as in **about**, **chicken**, **pencil**, **cannon**, **circus**	**t͟h** as in **there**
i as in **it**	**o͞o** as in **too**		**zh** as in **treasure**
ī as in **kite**	**or** as in **form**		

The mark (´) is placed after a syllable with a heavy accent, as in **chicken** (chik´ ən).

The mark (´) after a syllable shows a lighter accent, as in **disappear** (dis´ ə pēr´).

A

acorn (ā´ korn) *n.* The nut of the oak tree.

action (ak´ shən) *n.* The process of doing something.

admirers (ad mīr´ ərz) *n.* Plural form of **admirer:** A person who highly respects another person or thing.

adored (ə dord´) *v.* Past tense of **adore:** To love.

aerial (âr´ ē əl) *adj.* In or of the air.

album (al´ bəm) *n.* A book with blank pages in which photos and other personal items are kept.

angry (ang´ grē) *adj.* Very upset.

approached (ə prōchd´) *v.* Past tense of **approach:** To come near.

assured (ə shûrd´) *v.* Past tense of **assure:** To give confidence to.

asthma (az´ mə) *n.* A disease that makes it difficult to breathe and causes wheezing and coughing.

B

balcony (bal´ kə nē) *n.* A platform that sticks out from a building and has a low wall or railing on three sides.

batter (ba´ tər) *n.* A mixture used for cooking.

beautiful (bū´ tə fəl) *adj.* Pleasing to look at, hear, or think about.

blue (blo͞o) *adj.* Unhappy; sad.

bought (bôt) *v.* Past tense of **buy:** To purchase.

bridle (brī´ dəl) *n.* The part of a horse's harness that fits over the animal's head and is used to guide the horse.

brook (brŏŏk) *n.* A small stream.

brush (brush) *n.* Cut or broken twigs or branches.

burst (bûrst) *v.* To suddenly break out.

C

calmly (käm´ lē) *adv.* Without excitement; quietly.

clever (klev´ ər) *adj.* Mentally sharp; bright and alert.

coaches (kōch´ əz) *n.* Plural form of **coach:** A large, closed carriage pulled by horses with seats inside for passengers and a raised seat outside for the driver.

cocoon (kə kōōn´) *n.* The protective case that encloses certain insects while they develop into adulthood.

collect (kə lekt´) *v.* To gather together.

commented (ko´ men təd) *v.* Past tense of **comment:** To make a statement or remark.

communicate (kə mū´ ni kāt´) *v.* To pass along information, thoughts, or feelings.

complaining (kəm plān´ ing) A form of the verb **complain:** To find fault.

coward (kou´ ərd) *n.* Someone who is easily frightened.

crooked (krŏŏk´ id) *adj.* Not straight.

crouched (krouchd) *v.* Past tense of **crouch:** To stoop or bend low with the knees bent.

cupboard (kub´ ərd) *n.* A small cabinet or closet.

curious (kyûr´ ē əs) *adj.* Eager to know or learn.

D

describe (di scrīb´) *v.* To tell or write about.

desert (dez´ ərt) *n.* A hot, dry, sandy area of land with little or no plants growing on it.

deserted (di zûr´ ted) A form of the verb **desert:** To abandon.

dinnertime (din´ ər tīm´) *n.* The time when the main meal of the day is served.

dinosaur (dī´ nə sor´) *n.* Any of a group of extinct reptiles that lived long ago.

disappointed (dis´ ə poin´ ted) *adj.* Failed to meet hopes and expectations; frustrated.

discovery (dis kuv´ ə rē) *n.* Something learned for the first time.

disturb (di stûrb´) *v.* To bother or interfere.

Glossary

E

earn (ûrn) *v.* To get as a result of doing something.

empty (emp´ tē) *adj.* Having nothing within.

F

fabrics (fab´ riks) *n.* Plural form of **fabric**: A material that is woven or knitted from fibers.

fiesta (fē es´ tə) *n.* A festival or celebration, especially in Spanish-speaking countries.

followed (fol´ ōd) *v.* Past tense of **follow**: To go or come after.

fortune (for´ chən) *n.* Great wealth; riches.

fragments (frag´ mənts) *n.* Plural form of **fragment**: A part broken off; a small piece.

frightened (frī´ tənd) A form of the verb **frighten**: To scare.

G

gopher (gō´ fər) *n.* A burrowing rodent.

H

hatched (hachd) *v.* Past tense of **hatch**: To come out of an egg.

I

instead (in sted´) *adv.* In place of another person or thing.

interesting (in´ tris ting) *adj.* Causing or holding attention.

interrupted (in´ tə rup´ ted) *v.* Past tense of **interrupt**: To stop a person who is acting or speaking.

invited (in vī´ ted) *v.* Past tense of **invite**: To request that someone go somewhere or do something.

J

jackal (jak´ əl) *n.* A wild dog with a pointed face and bushy tail.

K

kneeled (nēld) *v.* Past tense of **kneel**: To go down on bent knee or knees.

knit (nit) *v.* To make cloth or garments by using needles to loop yarn together.

L

liberated (lib´ ə rā´ ted) A form of the verb **liberate**: To set free.

location (lō kā´ shən) *n.* The exact place.

M

make-believe (māk´ bi lēv´) *n.* Fantasy; imagination.

meadow (med´ ō) *n.* A piece of grassy land.

meanwhile (mēn´ hwīl´) *adv.* In or during the time between.

misfortune (mis for´ chən) *n.* Bad luck.

mountains (moun´ tənz) *n.* Plural form of **mountain:** A mass of land rising very high above the surrounding area.

N

nest (nest) *n.* A warm and comfortable place; a shelter.

O

outsmarted (out´ smär´ ted) *v.* Past tense of **outsmart:** To trick.

P

peddler (ped´ lər) *n.* A person who goes from place to place to sell something.

phrase (frāz) *n.* A brief expression or thought.

piloted (pī´ lə tid) *v.* Past tense of **pilot:** To steer or guide.

plumes (plo͞omz) *n.* Plural form of **plume:** A large, fluffy feather.

posies (pō´ zēz) *n.* Plural form of **posy:** A flower or bunch of flowers.

predawn (prē dôn´) *n.* Before daybreak.

prey (prā) *n.* Any animal hunted or killed by another animal for food.

purr (pûr) *v.* To make a soft, murmuring sound.

Q

queasy (kwē´ zē) *adj.* Feeling sick to one's stomach.

R

rapped (rapt) *v.* Past tense of **rap:** To tap or knock sharply.

recent (rē´ sənt) *adj.* Done, made, or happening just before the present time.

relief (ri lēf´) *n.* Comfort.

roared (rord) *v.* Past tense of **roar:** To shout or express loudly.

S

salmon (sam´ ən) *n.* A fish that typically lives in salt water and has a large, silver body with a dark back and yellowish–pink flesh.

scamper (skam´ pər) *v.* To run or flee quickly.

shortly (short´ lē) *adv.* Soon.

silvery (sil´ və rē) *adj.* Having the shiny whiteness of silver.

snatched (snachd) *v.* Past tense of **snatch:** To grab quickly.

spare (spâr) *adj.* Extra.

spoil (spoil) *v.* To ruin.

squawked (skwôkd) *v.* Past tense of **squawk:** To make a shrill, harsh cry, as a parrot.

squeaked (skwēkd) *v.* Past tense of **squeak:** To make a short, high-pitched sound.

Glossary

stamped (stampt) A form of the verb **stamp**: To mark.

streaked (strēkd) *v.* Past tense of **streak**: To move, run, or go at a great speed.

strolling (strōl´ ing) A form of the verb **stroll**: To walk in a slow, relaxed way.

structure (struk´ chər) *n.* Anything that is built, such as a building or a bridge.

stunned (stund) A form of the verb **stun**: To shock.

substance (sub´ stəns) *n.* A kind of material.

sure (shûr) *adj.* Steady.

T

tagging (tag´ ing) A form of the verb **tag**: To follow closely.

tearing (târ´ ing) A form of the verb **tear**: To pull apart or into pieces.

thought (thôt) *v.* Past tense of **think**: To form ideas and make decisions.

thoughtful (thôt´ fəl) *adj.* Considerate.

tinder box (tin´ dər boks´) *n.* A box that holds materials used to start a fire.

toil (toil) *v.* To do hard and exhausting work.

totem poles (tō´ təm pōlz´) *n.* Plural form of **totem pole**: Among certain Native American tribes, a pole carved and painted with animals, plants, or objects that symbolize certain families or clans.

treasure (trezh´ ər) *n.* A valuable thing, such as money, jewels, or gold.

tremendous (tri men´ dəs) *adj.* Of great intensity.

trudged (trujd) *v.* Past tense of **trudge**: To walk in a steady, slow way.

trunks (trungkz) *n.* Plural form of **trunk**: The main stem of a tree from which branches grow.

trusty (trus´ tē) *adj.* Reliable.

V

valuable (val´ ū ə bəl) *adj.* Of great worth.

voyage (voi´ ij) *n.* A journey.

W

winding (wīn´ ding) *adj.* Full of bends or turns.

wrecked (rekd) A form of the verb **wreck**: To destroy or ruin.

206